The Sainsbury Book of
ENTERTAINING
Wendy Godfrey

D1422473

CONTENTS

Published exclusively for
J Sainsbury plc
Stamford Street, London SE1 9LL
by Cathay Books
59 Grosvenor Street, London W1

First published 1982
Reprinted 1983, 1984, 1985

© Cathay Books 1982
ISBN 0 86178 163 5

Printed in Hong Kong

INTRODUCTION

To be a successful hostess, preparation must start well in advance and attention paid to the food, wine, table setting and guest list. A good mixture of guests is essential to the success of any party.

When planning the menu, choose dishes using foods in season. This helps keep the cost down, and ensures that it will be easier to obtain quality ingredients. Think about the visual impact of the menu: has it variety of flavours, colours, textures, shapes? Choose one spectacular course to impress your guests and keep the other dishes simple – for convenience. Prepare as much as possible in advance, making full use of the freezer if you have one.

The choice of wines to accompany a meal is much easier nowadays. Foreign travel and ethnic restaurants have increased the popularity of table wines and there are no strict rules of which wine to serve with which food – offer a selection if you can.

Don't overlook the importance of the table setting as it enhances the appearance of the food. Cutlery and glass should be gleaming and flowers must be fresh. One simple bloom is often enough for a small table; more spectacular arrangements can be used for a buffet table or around the house.

Plan carefully and well in advance and you can relax and enjoy your party as much as your guests.

NOTES

Standard spoon measurements are used in all recipes
1 tablespoon = one 15 ml spoon
1 teaspoon = one 5 ml spoon
All spoon measures are level.

Fresh herbs are used unless otherwise stated. If unobtainable substitute a bouquet garni of the equivalent dried herbs, or use dried herbs instead but halve the quantities stated.

Use freshly ground black pepper where pepper is specified.

Ovens should be preheated to the specified temperature.

For all recipes, quantities are given in both metric and imperial measures. Follow either set but not a mixture of both, because they are not interchangeable.

Menu suggestions are given at the beginning of each chapter. Those marked with an asterisk are economical menus.

COCKTAIL PARTIES

Drinks and savouries are the best way to give a large party successfully without worrying too much about fluctuating numbers. Cocktails are evocative of a time when drinks were more important than food, but by providing a selection of tasty savouries, the emphasis can be changed.

Allow approximately five savouries per person, as well as crisps and nuts. Prepare all the food in advance so that only reheating needs to be done at the last moment. Very often at this type of party, guests come and go and prior preparation of food allows the hostess to relax and enjoy herself as well.

All the food should be able to be picked up easily by hand and in bite size pieces. Cheese pastry makes an excellent base, cut in different shapes and sizes, for a range of toppings. Mini-cocktail sausages are a perennial favourite, as are cubes of cheeses speared on cocktail sticks with cocktail onions or pieces of fresh fruit or vegetable. Arrange the food on small tables around the room, replenishing as necessary.

Many of the recipes in this chapter are also ideal for serving with aperitifs before a dinner party – guests always appreciate a little extra effort made on their behalf.

Drinks are best restricted to ready-mixed cocktails and wine, or sherry. Fruit drinks or mineral waters should also be provided for those who don't like alcoholic drinks. As well as preparing food ahead, ice cubes can also be made up in advance. Freeze them in trays and then transfer the ice cubes to a large freezer bag so that plenty are available for the party. Allow three to five drinks per person.

Cocktail parties

Walnut dip
Avocado and cheese
savoury
Tapenade
Sage cream
Chive biscuits
Cheese biscuits
Spiced almonds
Devils on horseback
Tuna and parmesan
puffs
Baby pizzas
Lamb and mint
meatballs
Satay with peanut sauce

Bronx cocktail
Salty dog
Manhattan cocktail
Cool passion

Walnut Dip

125 g (4 oz) walnut
  pieces
1 clove garlic
1 tablespoon olive oil
1 teaspoon lemon
  juice
250 g (8 oz) natural
  low-fat yogurt
salt and pepper
¼ cucumber, peeled

Put the walnut pieces, garlic, oil and
lemon juice in an electric blender and
work until smooth. Add the yogurt
and blend in quickly. Season with
salt and pepper to taste.

Transfer to a serving bowl. Chop
the cucumber finely and stir into the
dip. Serve chilled, with crisp fresh
vegetables or biscuits.
Makes about 450 ml (¾ pint)

Avocado and Cheese Savoury

2 avocado pears
1 tablespoon lemon
  juice
2 tomatoes, skinned,
  seeded and chopped
2 cloves garlic, crushed
½ onion, grated
1 × 62.5 g (2.2 oz)
  packet creamy soft
  cheese
salt and pepper

Peel the avocados, halve and remove
the stones, then mash with the lemon
juice. Beat in the remaining
ingredients, with salt and pepper to
taste.

Serve as a dip with Chive or
Cheese Biscuits (see page 10) or crisps.
Makes about 300 ml (½ pint)

Tapenade

150 g (5 oz) stuffed
  green olives
1 × 100 g (3½ oz) can
  tuna fish, drained
1 × 50 g (1¾ oz) can
  anchovies, drained
3 tablespoons capers
2 teaspoons lemon juice
150 ml (¼ pint)
  olive oil
1 tablespoon brandy
Dijon mustard
pepper

Reserve a few olives for garnish,
slicing them finely. Put the rest of
the olives and the remaining
ingredients, with mustard and
pepper to taste, in an electric blender
and work until smooth.

Pour into a serving bowl and
garnish with the sliced olives. Serve
as a dip with Chive or Cheese
Biscuits (see page 10).

Makes about 450 ml (¾ pint)

Sage Cream

125 g (4 oz) each
  Sage Derby and
  curd cheese
4 tablespoons natural
  low-fat yogurt
salt and pepper
green food colouring
  (optional)

Beat the ingredients together until
smooth, with salt and pepper to taste,
and a few drops of colouring if liked.

Serve as a dip; pipe onto Chive or
Cheese Biscuits (see page 10), or into
pieces of celery; or use to sandwich
grape halves together.

Makes about 250 g (8 oz)

Spiced Almonds

3 tablespoons
    sunflower oil
125 g (4 oz) flaked
    almonds
1 teaspoon salt
1 teaspoon curry
    powder

Heat the oil in a frying pan, add the almonds and fry until golden brown. Drain on kitchen paper, then place in a serving dish.

Mix the salt and curry powder together and sprinkle over the almonds; toss well to coat.
Makes 125 g (4 oz)

Cheese Biscuits

125 g (4 oz) plain
    flour
50 g (2 oz) butter
50 g (2 oz) Cheddar
    cheese, grated
1 egg yolk
2 teaspoons cold
    water

Sift the flour into a bowl. Rub in the butter until the mixture resembles breadcrumbs, then stir in the cheese. Add the egg yolk and water and mix to a firm dough.

Turn onto a lightly floured board, roll out to a 5 mm (¼ inch) thickness and cut into 3.5 cm (1½ inch) rounds with a plain cutter. Place well apart on greased baking sheets and bake in a preheated moderately hot oven, 200°C (400°F), Gas Mark 6, for 10 minutes. Cool on a wire rack.

Serve on their own or with dips, or use as a base for savoury spreads.
Makes about 50

Chive Biscuits

125 g (4 oz) butter
2 × 62.5 g (2.2 oz)
    packets creamy soft
    cheese
125 g (4 oz) plain
    flour, sifted
1 tablespoon chopped
    chives

Cream the butter and cheese together until well blended. Stir in the flour and chives and mix with a fork until well combined. Roll the dough into a ball and wrap in cling film. Chill in the refrigerator for at least 1 hour.

Roll out to a 5 mm (¼ inch) thickness and cut into 3.5 cm (1½ inch) rounds with a plain cutter. Place well apart on greased baking sheets and bake in a preheated hot oven, 220°C (425°F), Gas Mark 7, for 10 minutes. Cool on a wire rack.

Serve on their own or with dips, or use as a base for savoury spreads.
Makes about 100

Devils on Horseback

25 g (1 oz) butter
1 onion, finely
    chopped
1 teaspoon dried sage
50 g (2 oz) fresh
    breadcrumbs
250 g (8 oz) prunes,
    stoned
10 streaky bacon
    rashers, derinded

Melt the butter in a pan, add the onion and fry gently until soft. Stir in the sage and breadcrumbs. Stuff the prunes with this mixture.

Stretch the bacon with the back of a knife, then cut each rasher in half. Wrap each prune in a piece of bacon and secure with a wooden cocktail stick. Grill for 4 to 5 minutes on each side, until the bacon is crisp.
Makes 20

11

Tuna and Parmesan Puffs

150 ml (¼ pint)
  water
50 g (2 oz) butter
75 g (3 oz) plain
  flour, sifted
2 eggs, beaten
25 g (1 oz) grated
  Parmesan cheese
FILLING:
1 × 198 g (7 oz) can
  tuna fish, drained
6 tablespoons
  mayonnaise
TO GARNISH:
parsley sprigs

Heat the water and butter slowly in a pan until the butter has melted. Remove from heat, quickly add all the flour and beat until the mixture leaves the side of the pan. Add the egg a little at a time, beating thoroughly between each addition. Beat in the cheese.

Spoon the mixture into a piping bag fitted with a 1 cm (½ inch) plain nozzle and pipe tiny mounds onto a dampened baking sheet, spacing them well apart. Bake in a preheated moderately hot oven, 200°C (400°F), Gas Mark 6, for 12 to 15 minutes, until crisp and golden.

Make a small slit in the side of each puff. Mash the tuna with the mayonnaise and spoon a little into each. Serve warm, garnished with parsley.
Makes about 150

Baby Pizzas

½ × 567 g (20 oz)
  packet white or
  brown bread mix
2 tablespoons oil
2 onions, finely
  chopped
2 cloves garlic, crushed
1 × 793 g (1 lb 12 oz)
  can tomatoes
1 × 142 g (5 oz)
  can tomato purée
2 teaspoons dried
  mixed herbs
salt and pepper
TO GARNISH:
1 × 50 g (1¾ oz)
  can anchovy
  fillets, drained
50 g (2 oz) small
  black olives,
  stoned and sliced
chopped parsley

Make up the bread mix following packet instructions and leave to rise.

Heat the oil in a frying pan, add the onions and garlic and fry gently until soft. Chop the tomatoes and add to the pan, with their juice, the tomato purée, herbs, and salt and pepper to taste. Simmer until the mixture begins to thicken.

Roll out the bread dough to a 5 mm (¼ inch) thickness and cut into 6 cm (2½ inch) rounds with a plain cutter. Place well apart on greased baking sheets and divide the tomato mixture between the pizzas. Bake in a preheated hot oven, 220°C (425°F), Gas Mark 7, for 10 to 15 minutes, until risen and golden.

Top each pizza with a circle of anchovy fillet, an olive slice and parsley. Serve hot or cold.
Makes about 50

Lamb and Mint Meatballs

500 g (1 lb) minced
　　lamb
2 cloves garlic, crushed
2 teaspoons mint
　　sauce
salt and pepper
1 egg, beaten
oil for shallow frying
PIQUANT DIP:
50 g (2 oz) demerara
　　sugar
2 teaspoons cornflour
3 tablespoons water
4 tablespoons
　　redcurrant jelly
2 tablespoons
　　Worcestershire
　　sauce
TO GARNISH:
parsley sprigs

Put the lamb in a bowl and add the
garlic and mint sauce. Season well
with salt and pepper and bind the
mixture with the egg. With floured
hands, roll into walnut-sized balls.

Heat the oil in a frying pan, add
the meatballs in batches and fry for
about 10 minutes until golden
brown. Drain on kitchen paper and
keep warm.

To make the dip, put the sugar,
cornflour and water in a small pan
and blend in the redcurrant jelly and
Worcestershire sauce. Bring slowly
to the boil and cook, stirring, until
smooth.

Spear the meatballs onto cocktail
sticks. Garnish with parsley and
serve warm, with the dip.
Makes about 25

Satay with Peanut Sauce

350 g (12 oz) pork
    fillet
1 teaspoon chilli
    powder
1 teaspoon water
1 tablespoon
    sunflower oil
1 onion, grated
1 clove garlic, crushed
2 tablespoons lemon
    juice
5 tablespoons water
4 tablespoons crunchy
    peanut butter
1 teaspoon salt
1 teaspoon cumin
    powder
1 teaspoon coriander
    powder

Cut the pork fillet into small dice and thread 3 or 4 pieces on one end of wooden cocktail sticks. Cook under a preheated hot grill for 1 minute on each side or until cooked through. Drain on kitchen paper and keep warm.

Blend the chilli powder and water together to make a paste. Heat the oil in a pan, add the onion, garlic and chilli paste and fry gently until the onion is soft. Add the remaining ingredients, stirring well to combine. Transfer to a serving bowl.

Serve the satay warm with the peanut sauce.

Makes about 20

NOTE: Garnish the satay with lemon slices and parsley if liked.

Cool Passion

1 × 500 ml (17.6 fl oz) carton orange and passionfruit juice
1 × 1 litre (1.76 pint) carton pineapple juice
1 × 1½ litre (50 fl oz) bottle lemonade
crushed ice

Pour the two fruit juices into a large jug and stir well to mix.

Just before serving, stir in the lemonade. Pour into glasses containing a little crushed ice.
Makes about 20 glasses

Bronx Cocktail

juice of 1 orange
300 ml (½ pint) gin
300 ml (½ pint) dry vermouth
300 ml (½ pint) sweet vermouth
ice cubes to serve

Put all the ingredients, except the ice cubes, in a large container with a tight-fitting lid. Shake well to mix. Strain into a serving jug and pour into glasses, containing a few ice cubes.
Makes 15 to 20 glasses

Salty Dog

150 ml (¼ pint) vodka
150 ml (¼ pint) grapefruit juice
1 egg white
25 g (1 oz) table salt
ice cubes to serve

Pour the vodka and grapefruit juice into a jug and stir well. Lightly whisk the egg white and pour onto a plate. Put the salt on another plate. Dip the rim of each glass in the egg white, then in the salt. Half-fill the glasses with ice and pour over the cocktail.
Makes about 8 glasses
NOTE: Equal quantities of vodka and orange juice in an unsalted glass is a 'Screwdriver'.

Manhattan Cocktail

150 ml (¼ pint) rye whisky
150 ml (¼ pint) dry vermouth
½ teaspoon Angostura bitters
1 teaspoon Curaçao (optional)
crushed ice

Put the liquid ingredients and ice in a cocktail shaker or a container with a tight-fitting lid. Shake well to mix. Strain into glasses to serve.
Makes about 8 glasses

DINNER PARTIES

A dinner party is the most intimate and formal type of entertaining – an event never to be rushed. A dinner for two presupposes a very special reason for celebrating, so the atmosphere must be thought about carefully. The mood of the evening should not be spoiled by jumping up from the table to supervise last-minute details. It is very easy to have two of the three courses ready prepared and one keeping warm in a low oven or a heated trolley.

At a small dinner party it's nice to serve something a little out of the ordinary, but not every course has to be complicated. Before planning the menu, check whether any of the guests has a personal dislike or a dietary veto on any food. With a small number around a table it can be embarrassing to have a refusal of something which has been carefully cooked. These menus serve two or six – simply increase or lessen the quantities for four.

With fewer people it is also possible to serve better quality wines which can be appreciated whilst sitting around a dinner table. A glass of sweet wine with the dessert also helps to give a grand finale to the meal.

Menu 1 for two

Pears with blue cheese dressing

Fillet steak en croûte
Stuffed tomatoes
Spinach and fennel salad

Crème brulée

Menu 2 for two

Smoked haddock mousse

Duck with grape sauce
Petits pois nests
Watercress, courgette
and tomato salad

Orange sorbet

Menu 3 for six

Individual fish flans

Guard of honour with
peppercorn sauce
Baked sliced potatoes
French beans with garlic

Strawberry ice cream

Menu 4 for six

Mushrooms à la
Grècque

Tongue with sherry
sauce
Nutty potatoes
Chinese leaves

Summer pudding

Menu 5 for six

Chilled lemon soup

Salmon koulibiac
Broccoli with
hollandaise
Leeks with bacon

Chocolate and rum
charlotte

Menu 6 for six

Almond roulade

Pork chops with
barbecue sauce
Courgette chips
Duchesse potatoes

Gooseberry ginger
crunch

Menu 7 for six★

Cheesy liver pâté

Veal blanquette
Mixed vegetable purée
Baked potatoes

Apple amber

Menu 8 for six

Ceviche

Victorian chicken pie
Ratatouille
French-style peas

Fruit meringue baskets

Pears with Blue Cheese Dressing

2 ripe pears
2 teaspoons lemon
   juice
125 g (4 oz) Danish
   Blue cheese
150 g (5 oz) natural
   low-fat yogurt
salt and pepper
TO GARNISH:
4 lettuce leaves,
   shredded
2 mint sprigs
	Peel the pears, keeping the stalks on. Carefully remove the cores, using a teaspoon. Brush the pears with lemon juice to prevent discoloration. Cream the cheese until soft and use 25 g (1 oz) to stuff each pear. Add the yogurt to the remaining cheese and blend well. Season with salt and pepper to taste.
	   Arrange the lettuce on 2 small plates and stand a pear on each. Carefully coat with the blue cheese dressing and garnish the top of each pear with mint leaves.
	Serves 2

Smoked Haddock Mousse

175 g (6 oz) smoked
   haddock
120 ml (4 fl oz)
   milk
1 bay leaf
15 g (½ oz) butter
1 tablespoon plain
   flour
1 tablespoon lemon
   juice
4 tablespoons double
   cream
salt and pepper
few cucumber slices
   to garnish
	Put the haddock, milk and bay leaf in a saucepan. Bring to the boil, cover and simmer for 10 minutes. Strain and reserve the milk; flake the fish.
	   Melt the butter in a saucepan and blend in the flour. Gradually add the reserved milk and bring to the boil, stirring, until thickened.
	   Remove from the heat and stir in the lemon juice, then fold in the flaked fish. Whisk the cream until thick and fold into the mixture. Season with salt and pepper to taste.
	   Transfer to 2 ramekin dishes and chill until required. Garnish with cucumber slices to serve.
	Serves 2

Individual Fish Flans

PASTRY:
*225 g (8 oz) plain
  flour*
*125 g (4 oz) butter
  or margarine*
*2-3 tablespoons iced
  water*

FILLING:
*6 small plaice fillets,
  skinned*
*300 ml (½ pint)
  milk*
salt and pepper
*125 g (4 oz) peeled
  prawns*
25 g (1 oz) butter
*25 g (1 oz) plain
  flour*
*2 tablespoons
  chopped parsley*
1 egg yolk

Sift the flour into a bowl. Rub in the butter or margarine until the mixture resembles breadcrumbs. Add the water gradually and mix to a firm dough.

Turn out onto a floured surface and knead lightly. Roll out and use to line six 7.5 cm (3 inch) flan rings. Line with greaseproof paper and dried beans and bake in a preheated moderately hot oven, 200°C (400°F), Gas Mark 6, for 10 minutes. Remove the paper and beans and return to the oven for 5 minutes. Remove the flan rings and cool on a wire rack.

Roll up the plaice fillets and place in a buttered ovenproof dish with 4 tablespoons of the milk. Season with salt and pepper to taste and cover with buttered paper. Cook in a preheated hot oven, 220°C (425°F), Gas Mark 7, for 10 minutes.

Divide the prawns between the flan cases. Transfer the cooked plaice with a slotted spoon to the flan cases; reserve the cooking juices.

Melt the butter in a small pan, stir in the flour then gradually add the remaining milk and reserved cooking juices. Bring to the boil, then add the parsley and salt and pepper to taste. Cool slightly and beat in the egg yolk.

Spoon the hot sauce over the fish in the flan cases and place under a preheated moderate grill until golden brown. Serve immediately.
Serves 6

Mushrooms à la Grècque

2 tablespoons olive oil
1 onion, finely
    chopped
1 clove garlic, crushed
500 g (1 lb) button
    mushrooms
150 ml (¼ pint) dry
    white wine
2 tablespoons tomato
    purée
1 teaspoon sugar
1 bouquet garni
salt and pepper
chopped parsley to
    garnish

Heat the oil in a pan, add the onion
and garlic and fry gently until
translucent. Add the mushrooms and
remaining ingredients, with salt and
pepper to taste. Cook, uncovered,
for 20 minutes. Leave to cool, then
remove the bouquet garni.

Transfer to a serving dish and chill
until required. Sprinkle with
chopped parsley and serve with crisp
warm rolls.
Serves 6

Chilled Lemon Soup

25 g (1 oz) butter
1 onion, chopped
25 g (1 oz) plain
  flour
2 large lemons
900 ml (1½ pints)
  chicken stock
150 ml (¼ pint)
  milk
salt and pepper
TO GARNISH:
6 tablespoons double
  cream, lightly
  whipped

Melt the butter in a pan, add the onion and fry gently until translucent, but not brown. Stir in the flour. Thinly pare the rind from 1 lemon and add to the pan with the stock and milk. Bring slowly to the boil, stirring constantly, then simmer for 5 minutes.

Finely grate the rind from the other lemon and keep on one side. Squeeze the juice from both lemons and add to the soup. Cool, strain and season lightly with salt and pepper. Chill well.

To serve, pour into individual bowls, top each with a tablespoon of cream and sprinkle with the grated lemon rind.

Serves 6

NOTE: This soup can also be served hot: stir the grated lemon rind into the soup and serve with croûtons.

Almond Roulade

3 eggs, separated
25 g (1 oz) light soft
 brown sugar
½ teaspoon salt
125 g (4 oz) ground
 almonds
FILLING:
125 g (4 oz) peeled
 prawns
300 ml (½ pint)
 mayonnaise
1 tablespoon chopped
 parsley
1 tablespoon chopped
 capers
1 tablespoon chopped
 gherkins
salt and pepper
TO GARNISH:
shredded lettuce

Put the egg yolks in a warm bowl
and whisk for 5 minutes. Add the
sugar and salt and whisk for 7 minutes. Whisk the egg whites until
stiff, then fold into the egg yolk
mixture. Finally fold in the almonds.

Turn into a 30 × 20 cm (12 × 8
inch) Swiss roll tin lined with oiled
silicone paper, spreading the mixture
into the corners. Bake in a preheated
moderate oven, 180°C (350°F), Gas
Mark 4, for 12 to 15 minutes, until
firm and lightly browned. Turn out
onto a sheet of greaseproof paper and
carefully remove the paper. Leave
until cold.

Mix all the filling ingredients
together, adding salt and pepper to
taste.

When the roulade is cold, spread
with the filling and roll up like a
Swiss roll. Serve garnished with
shredded lettuce.

Serves 6

Cheesy Liver Pâté

150 g (5 oz) liver
   sausage
227 g (8 oz) soft
   creamy cheese
2 cloves garlic,
   crushed
1 tablespoon chopped
   parsley

Beat all the ingredients together until soft. Transfer to a serving bowl and serve with toasted brown bread.

Serves 6

VARIATIONS:

1. Sauté 25 g (1 oz) chopped button mushrooms in 1 tablespoon oil until softened. Drain and stir into the pâté before serving.

2. Sauté one finely chopped onion in 1 tablespoon oil until soft. Drain and combine with the other ingredients.

Ceviche

500 g (1 lb) monk
   fish or any firm
   white fish
juice of 2 lemons
4 tomatoes, skinned,
   seeded and diced
1 green pepper,
   cored, seeded and
   diced
4 tablespoons olive
   oil
1 tablespoon white
   wine vinegar
2 tablespoons
   chopped parsley
salt and pepper
TO GARNISH:
1 small lettuce
1 avocado pear,
   peeled and sliced
6 black olives, stoned
   and sliced

Remove the skin and bones from the fish and cut the flesh into dice. Put into a basin and pour over the lemon juice. Leave to marinate for at least 3 hours, preferably overnight.

Add the tomatoes and green pepper to the fish with the remaining ingredients, seasoning with salt and pepper to taste. Stir well to mix.

Line 6 individual plates with lettuce leaves. Divide the mixture into 6 portions and pile on top of the lettuce. Garnish with avocado and olive slices.

Serves 6

Fillet Steak en Croûte

2 fillet steaks, 2.5 cm
 (1 inch) thick
 (approximately)
pepper
75 g (3 oz)
 Ardennes pâté
1 × 215 g (7½ oz)
 packet frozen puff
 pastry, thawed
beaten egg to glaze

Sprinkle the steaks with pepper and put under a hot grill for 1 minute on each side. Cool and spread with pâté.

Cut the pastry in half and roll out each piece to a 5 mm (¼ inch) thickness. Wrap the steak in the pastry, with the join underneath. Decorate the top with shapes cut from the pastry trimmings and brush with beaten egg.

Bake in a preheated hot oven, 220°C (425°F), Gas Mark 7, for 15 to 20 minutes, until golden brown. Serve immediately.
Serves 2

Stuffed Tomatoes

2 large tomatoes
15 g (½ oz) butter
1 small onion,
 chopped
4 tablespoons fresh
 breadcrumbs
1 tablespoon
 horseradish sauce
1 tablespoon chopped
 parsley
salt and pepper
watercress sprigs to
 garnish

Cut a slice from the top of each tomato and scoop out the pulp.

Melt the butter in a pan, add the onion and fry until soft. Stir in the breadcrumbs, horseradish, parsley and chopped tomato pulp. Season liberally with salt and pepper.

Fill the tomato shells with the mixture and bake in a preheated moderately hot oven, 200°C (400°F), Gas Mark 6, for 15 to 20 minutes. Serve hot, garnished with watercress.
Serves 2

Spinach and Fennel Salad

125 g (4 oz) small
 spinach leaves
1 fennel bulb
50 g (2 oz) walnut
 pieces
2 tablespoons French
 dressing

Remove any thick stalks from the spinach and tear the leaves into a salad bowl.

Trim the leaves from the fennel and reserve. Slice the fennel and add to the bowl with the walnuts.

Just before serving, pour over the dressing and toss well to coat. Garnish with fennel leaves.
Serves 2

Crispy Duck with Grape Sauce

2 duck portions
1 teaspoon salt
1 teaspoon arrowroot
150 ml (¼ pint)
orange juice
125 g (4 oz) black
grapes, halved and
seeded
TO GARNISH:
1 orange, sliced
2 watercress sprigs

Sprinkle the duck portions with the salt. Place on a rack in a roasting pan and cook in a preheated hot oven, 230°C (450°F), Gas Mark 8, for 30 minutes.

Meanwhile, blend the arrowroot with the orange juice in a small pan. Bring to the boil, then stir in the grapes.

Transfer the duck to a warmed serving dish and pour over the sauce. Garnish with orange slices and watercress to serve.
Serves 2

Watercress, Courgette and Tomato Salad

½ bunch watercress
1 courgette, thinly
  sliced
2 tomatoes, sliced
2 tablespoons French
  dressing

Mix the vegetables together in a salad bowl. Just before serving, pour over the French dressing and toss well to coat.
Serves 2

Petits Pois Nests

350 g (12 oz)
  potatoes, boiled
25 g (1 oz) butter
2 tablespoons milk
1 egg, beaten
1 × 113 g (4 oz)
  packet frozen
  petits pois

Mash the potatoes with the butter, milk and egg. Pipe into small nest shapes on a greased baking sheet and bake in a preheated moderately hot oven, 200°C (400°F), Gas Mark 6, for about 20 minutes, until golden brown.

Meanwhile, cook the petits pois in a little boiling salted water for 2 minutes; drain.

Transfer the potato nests to a warmed serving dish and fill with the peas. Serve hot.
Serves 2

Guard of Honour with Peppercorn Sauce

2 best end necks of
   lamb (6-7 cutlets
   each)
1 rosemary sprig
SAUCE:
25 g (1 oz) butter
2 rashers streaky
   bacon, derinded
   and chopped
1 small onion
50 g (2 oz)
   mushrooms
1 small carrot
25 g (1 oz) flour
300 ml (½ pint) beef
   stock
1 teaspoon dried
   mixed herbs
2 tablespoons tomato
   purée
salt and pepper
2 tablespoons sherry
2 tablespoons
   redcurrant jelly
2 tablespoons green
   peppercorns

For the sauce, melt the butter in a pan, add the bacon and fry for 2 minutes. Chop the vegetables, add to the pan and fry for 5 minutes. Stir in the flour, then gradually stir in the stock and bring to the boil. Add the herbs, tomato purée, and salt and pepper to taste. Cover and simmer for 1 hour.

Trim off the meat 5 cm (2 inches) from the tip of the lamb bones and scrape these tips clean. Sew the cutlets together to form an arch shape, using a trussing needle and fine string. Cover the tips with foil. Place the rosemary in the centre.

Roast in a preheated moderate oven, 180°C (350°F), Gas Mark 4, for about 1 hour, until tender.

Sieve the sauce into a clean pan and add the remaining ingredients. Heat through gently.

Remove the foil and replace with cutlet frills. Transfer the lamb to a warmed serving dish and serve with the sauce.
Serves 6

Baked Sliced Potatoes

1 kg (2 lb) potatoes,
   thinly sliced
125 g (4 oz) butter
salt and pepper
chopped parsley to
   garnish

Soak the potatoes in cold water to remove excess starch; dry thoroughly.

Butter a large, shallow ovenproof dish; melt the remaining butter in a small pan. Put a layer of potatoes in the bottom of the dish. Drizzle a little butter over and season lightly with salt and pepper. Repeat these layers, finishing with butter. Cover and cook in a preheated moderately hot oven, 200°C (400°F), Gas Mark 6, for 1 hour.

Sprinkle with chopped parsley and serve from the dish.
Serves 6

French Beans with Garlic

500 g (1 lb) French
   or dwarf beans, cut
   into 5 cm (2 inch)
   pieces
25 g (1 oz) butter
2 tablespoons oil
2 cloves garlic, sliced

Plunge the beans into boiling water for 1 minute; drain. Just before serving, heat the butter and oil and add the garlic. Fry for 1 minute then add the beans. Toss well and cook for 2 minutes, stirring frequently.

Transfer to a warmed serving dish and serve immediately.

Serves 6

Tongue with Sherry Sauce

1 cured ox tongue,
    about 1.5 kg
    (3½ lb)
1 onion
2 bay leaves
salt and pepper
SAUCE:
40 g (1½ oz) butter
40 g (1½ oz) plain
    flour
150 ml (¼ pint)
    sweet sherry
2 tablespoons
    redcurrant jelly
watercress sprigs to
    garnish

Soak the tongue overnight in cold water. Drain and put in a large pan, cover with cold water and bring to the boil. Boil for 5 minutes then drain again. Add fresh cold water to cover the tongue, the onion, bay leaves, and salt and pepper to taste. Bring to the boil and simmer for 2½ to 3 hours, skimming frequently.

Drain, reserving 150 ml (¼ pint) cooking liquid, and plunge into cold water. Remove skin and any bones. Slice the tongue thickly, arrange on a warmed serving dish and keep warm.

Melt the butter in a pan and stir in the flour. Gradually stir in the sherry and reserved cooking liquid. Bring to the boil and simmer for 5 minutes. Add the redcurrant jelly and check the seasoning.

Pour the sauce over the tongue and serve garnished with watercress.
Serves 6

Nutty Potatoes

1 kg (2 lb) potatoes,
  boiled
50 g (2 oz) butter
2 tablespoons milk
125 g (4 oz) chopped
  mixed nuts

Mash potatoes with the butter and milk; leave to cool. Shape into a roll and cut into 24 pieces. Using your hands, roll into balls then flatten into cakes. Coat with chopped nuts.

Place on a greased baking sheet and cook in a preheated moderate oven, 180°C (350°F), Gas Mark 4, for 20 minutes, until crisp and golden.

Serves 6

Chinese Leaves

1 head of Chinese
  leaves, shredded
salt
50 g (2 oz) butter
grated rind and juice
  of 1 orange
½ teaspoon grated
  nutmeg
chopped parsley to
  garnish

Cook the Chinese leaves in a little boiling salted water for 5 minutes. Drain well.

Put the butter, orange rind and juice, and nutmeg in the pan. Add the Chinese leaves and toss well.

Transfer to a warmed serving dish and serve hot, garnished with parsley.

Serves 6

Salmon Koulibiac

625 g (1¼ lb)
  salmon, fresh or
  frozen and thawed
6 tablespoons milk
salt and pepper
125 g (4 oz)
  mushrooms, sliced
1 large onion,
  chopped
75 g (3 oz) brown
  rice, cooked
1 tablespoon chopped
  parsley
1 × 370 g (13 oz)
  packet frozen puff
  pastry, thawed
beaten egg to glaze

Put the salmon in a pan with the milk and salt and pepper to taste. Bring to the boil, cover and simmer for 5 minutes. Leave to cool in the pan. Drain, reserving the liquid; flake the fish, discarding the skin and bones. Combine the salmon with the mushrooms, onion, rice and parsley to make the filling.

Roll out the pastry to 37 × 33 cm (15 × 13 inches) and trim edges. Cut into 2 strips, one 15 cm (6 inches), and one 18 cm (7 inches) wide. Put the narrower strip on a baking sheet and cover, to within 1.5 cm (¾ inch) of the edges, with the filling. Dampen the edges and cover with remaining pastry, sealing the edges. Decorate with leaves cut from trimmings.

Brush with egg and bake in a pre-heated moderately hot oven, 200°C (400°F), Gas Mark 6, for 30 minutes, until golden brown. Serve hot, with parsley sauce if liked.
Serves 6

Broccoli with Hollandaise

1 kg (2 lb) broccoli
salt and pepper
3 egg yolks
1 teaspoon caster
  sugar
1 tablespoon white
  wine vinegar,
  warmed
2 tablespoons lemon
  juice, warmed
175 g (6 oz) butter,
  melted

Cook the broccoli in boiling salted water for 10 minutes. Drain, place in a warmed serving dish and keep hot.

Put the egg yolks, sugar and a pinch each of salt and pepper in an electric blender. Work on high speed, trickling in the vinegar and lemon juice after 5 seconds. When absorbed, trickle in the warm melted butter, still on high speed.

Alternatively, put the egg yolks, sugar, salt and pepper in a basin over a pan of hot water. Stir in the vinegar and lemon juice, then gradually whisk in the warm melted butter.

Pour the sauce over the broccoli to serve.
Serves 6

Leeks with Bacon

50 g (2 oz) butter
125 g (4 oz) streaky
    bacon, derinded
    and chopped
1 kg (2 lb) leeks,
    sliced
pepper

Melt the butter in a saucepan, add the bacon and fry for 2 minutes. Add the leeks and pepper to taste, cover and simmer for 20 minutes, stirring occasionally to prevent sticking.

Transfer to a warmed serving dish and serve immediately.
Serves 6

Pork Chops with Barbecue Sauce

6 pork chops
salt and pepper
SAUCE:
2 tablespoons oil
1 onion, chopped
2 cloves garlic, crushed
2 tablespoons tomato
 purée
2 tablespoons red
 wine vinegar
3 tablespoons
 Worcestershire
 sauce
3 tablespoons clear
 honey
½ teaspoon chilli
 powder
½ teaspoon mustard
 powder
½ teaspoon salt
1 × 227 g (8 oz)
 can tomatoes
TO GARNISH:
parsley sprigs

Season the chops liberally with salt and pepper. Place in a large shallow ovenproof dish and cook in a preheated moderately hot oven, 190°C (375°F), Gas Mark 5, for 30 minutes. Drain off any excess fat and turn the chops over.

Meanwhile, make the sauce. Heat the oil in a pan, add the onion and garlic and fry gently until soft. Add the remaining ingredients, bring to the boil and simmer for 15 minutes. Pour over the chops and return to the oven for 20 minutes, until tender. Serve, garnished with parsley.
Serves 6

Courgette Chips

500 g (1 lb)
  courgettes
50 g (2 oz) plain
  flour
salt and pepper
oil for deep-frying

Cut the courgettes into chips. Season the flour with salt and pepper and put in a large polythene bag. Add the courgette chips and shake to coat well.

Heat the oil in a deep pan and fry the courgettes, in batches, for 5 minutes. Drain on kitchen paper; keep warm while cooking the remainder.

Just before serving, plunge once again into hot oil for 1 minute. Shake off excess oil and serve immediately.
Serves 6

Duchesse Potatoes

750 g (1½ lb)
  potatoes, boiled
75 g (3 oz) butter
1 egg, beaten
salt and pepper

Sieve or mash the potatoes and beat together with the butter, egg, and salt and pepper to taste. Put in a piping bag fitted with a large star nozzle and pipe into whirls on a baking sheet. Cook in a preheated moderately hot oven, 200°C (400°F), Gas Mark 6, for 20 minutes until crisp and golden.
Serves 6

Veal Blanquette

1 kg (2 lb) pie veal,
   cut into 2.5 cm
   (1 inch) cubes
2 onions, chopped
2 carrots, sliced
1 tablespoon lemon
   juice
2 bay leaves
salt and pepper
50 g (2 oz) butter
50 g (2 oz) plain
   flour
3 tablespoons single
   cream
TO GARNISH:
6 rashers streaky
   bacon, derinded
1 lemon, cut into
   wedges
parsley sprigs

Put the veal in a saucepan with the
vegetables, lemon juice, bay leaves,
and salt and pepper to taste. Add
enough water to cover and simmer,
covered, for 1½ hours. Remove the
meat and vegetables from the pan
with a slotted spoon and keep on one
side. Discard the bay leaf. Strain the
stock, reserving 600 ml (1 pint).

Melt the butter in the pan and stir
in the flour. Gradually add the
reserved stock and bring to the boil.
Remove from the heat and stir in the
cream. Check the seasoning and
return the meat and vegetables to the
pan. Heat through very gently while
preparing the garnish.

Roll up the bacon rashers tightly
and thread onto a skewer. Place
under a preheated hot grill until
crisp.

Transfer the veal to a warmed
serving dish and garnish with the
bacon rolls, lemon wedges and
parsley.
Serves 6

Mixed Vegetable Purée

500 g (1 lb) parsnips
500 g (1 lb) carrots
500 g (1 lb) Brussels
   sprouts
salt and pepper
150 ml (¼ pint)
   double cream
75 g (3 oz) butter
parsley sprigs to
   garnish

Cut the parsnips and carrots into
even-sized pieces. Cook the parsnips,
carrots and sprouts separately in
boiling salted water: parsnips for
20 minutes, carrots for 15 minutes
and sprouts for 8 minutes. Drain
well.

Sieve or blend each vegetable
separately with one-third of the
cream and one-third of the butter.
Season liberally with salt and pepper.

To serve, arrange in stripes in an
oblong dish or in sections in a round
dish. Garnish with parsley.
Serves 6
NOTE: Celeriac, kohl rabi and turnips
can be prepared in the same way.

Baked Potatoes

6 potatoes, each
weighing about
250 g (8 oz)
75 g (3 oz) butter
salt and pepper
chopped parsley to
garnish

Scrub the potatoes well and dry. Cut
a cross on one side of each. Rub all
over with butter paper and cook on
the rack in a preheated moderately
hot oven, 200°C (400°F), Gas Mark
6, for 1¼ hours. Push back the cut
skin to open up the cross and top
with 15 g (½ oz) butter. Sprinkle
with salt and pepper and chopped
parsley to serve.
Serves 6

Victorian Chicken Pie

50 g (2 oz) butter
50 g (2 oz)
  mushrooms, sliced
1 green pepper,
  cored, seeded and
  sliced
50 g (2 oz) plain
  flour
142 ml (5 fl oz)
  soured cream
150 ml (¼ pint)
  chicken stock
2 tablespoons sherry
½ teaspoon chilli
  powder
1 kg (2 lb) cooked
  chicken, cubed
salt and pepper
1 × 215 g (7½ oz)
  packet frozen puff
  pastry, thawed
beaten egg to glaze

Melt the butter in a saucepan, add the mushrooms and green pepper and fry gently until soft. Stir in the flour, then gradually add the soured cream, stock, sherry and chilli powder, stirring constantly. Bring to the boil, stirring, then fold in the chicken. Season to taste with salt and pepper and transfer to a 1.5 litre (2½ pint) pie dish.

Roll out the pastry thinly to 5 cm (2 inches) larger than the dish. Cut off a narrow strip all round and use to cover the dampened rim of the dish; brush with water. Cover the dish with the lid, sealing the edges well. Trim and flute the edges, make a hole in the centre and decorate with leaves cut from trimmings.

Brush with beaten egg and bake in a preheated moderately hot oven, 200°C (400°F), Gas Mark 6, for 25 to 30 minutes, until golden brown. Serve hot.
Serves 6

French-Style Peas

4 lettuce leaves
½ bunch spring onions
750 g (1½ lb)
   frozen peas
150 ml (¼ pint) water
1 teaspoon lemon
   juice
1 teaspoon sugar
50 g (2 oz) butter

Shred the lettuce and slice the spring onions. Put all the ingredients, except the butter, in a saucepan. Bring to the boil, cover and simmer for 8 minutes; drain.

Place in a warmed serving dish, dot with the butter and serve.
Serves 6

Ratatouille

3 tablespoons olive
   oil
2 onions, sliced
2 cloves garlic, crushed
1 aubergine, sliced
1 green pepper, cored,
   seeded and sliced
250 g (8 oz)
   courgettes, sliced
250 g (8 oz)
   tomatoes, skinned
   and sliced
salt and pepper

Heat the oil in a flameproof casserole, add the onion and garlic and fry gently until translucent. Add the aubergine and fry for 5 minutes, turning frequently. Add the remaining ingredients, seasoning liberally with salt and pepper. Stir well. Cover and cook in a preheated moderate oven, 180°C (350°F), Gas Mark 4, for 1 hour. Serve hot.
Serves 6
NOTE: This can also be served cold as a starter.

Crème Brulée

150 ml (¼ pint)
double cream
6 drops vanilla
essence
1 egg yolk
50 g (2 oz) caster
sugar

Place the cream and vanilla essence in a small pan and heat very gently. Whisk the egg yolk with 1 teaspoon of the sugar in a heatproof basin. Stir in the cream and stand the basin over a pan of simmering water. Stir constantly until the mixture thickens slightly.

Pour into 2 ramekin dishes and bake in a preheated moderate oven, 160°C (325°F), Gas Mark 3, for 8 minutes. Cool slightly, then place in the refrigerator until thoroughly chilled, preferably overnight.

Sprinkle evenly with the remaining sugar and place under a preheated hot grill until the sugar has caramelized. Cool, then chill for about 2 hours before serving.
Serves 2

Orange Sorbet

50 g (2 oz) caster
sugar
150 ml (¼ pint)
water
2 large oranges
1 teaspoon lemon
juice
1 egg white, whisked
shredded orange rind
to decorate

Place the sugar and water in a pan and heat gently, stirring until dissolved. Bring to the boil, simmer for 10 minutes, then leave to cool.

Cut off the tops of the oranges. Using a sharp knife, remove as much flesh from the insides as possible. Reserve the orange shells.

Add the flesh to the syrup with the lemon juice, then sieve into a rigid freezerproof container. Cover, seal and freeze for about 2 hours, until mushy.

Whisk the egg white into the orange mixture. Spoon into the orange shells and place them in a freezerproof container; freeze until firm.

Transfer to the refrigerator 1 hour before serving to soften. Decorate with shredded orange rind to serve.
Serves 2

Strawberry Ice Cream

4 egg yolks
½ × 340 g (12 oz)
  jar strawberry
  conserve
284 ml (10 fl oz)
  double cream
2 tablespoons brandy
  (optional)

Whisk the egg yolks in a warmed bowl for at least 5 minutes, until pale and thick. Add the conserve and whisk again.

Beat the cream, with the brandy if using, until it forms soft peaks. Fold into the strawberry mixture and turn into a rigid freezerproof container. Cover and freeze until firm.

Scoop into chilled individual dishes to serve.

Serves 6

Summer Pudding

500 g (1 lb) mixed
  soft fruit
  (raspberries,
  redcurrants,
  blackberries,
  strawberries,
  blackcurrants, etc.)
125 g (4 oz) caster
  sugar
6 thin slices white
  bread, crusts
  removed

Put the fruit in a saucepan with the
sugar and simmer gently, stirring
occasionally, for about 10 minutes,
until tender but not mushy.

Cut one circle of bread to fit the
base of a 900 ml (1½ pint) pudding
basin, one for the middle and one
to fit the top. Cut the remaining
bread in half lengthwise. Place the
small circle in the basin. Line the
sides with the slices of bread. Pour
in half of the fruit and cover with the
middle circle. Top with remaining
fruit, then the large circle of bread.

Put the basin on a plate, cover
with a saucer and put a weight on
top. Leave in a cool place overnight.

Turn out onto a serving plate and
serve with cream.

Serves 6

46

Chocolate and Rum Charlotte

1½ packets sponge
  fingers
4 tablespoons rum
100 g (3½ oz) plain
  chocolate
75 g (3 oz) light soft
  brown sugar
125 g (4 oz)
  unsalted butter,
  softened
2 eggs, separated
TO DECORATE:
rose leaves, washed
  and thoroughly
  dried
50 g (2 oz) plain
  chocolate, melted
150 ml (¼ pint)
  double cream,
  whipped

Dip each sponge finger into the rum and use to line the base and sides of an 18 cm (6 inch) soufflé dish, sugar side out.

Melt the chocolate in a basin over hot water. Cream the sugar and butter until light, then stir in the chocolate while still hot. Beat in the egg yolks, then fold in the stiffly whisked egg whites. Pour into the soufflé dish and chill for 24 hours.

To prepare the rose leaves, paint the underside of each with the melted chocolate. Leave until set, then carefully peel each leaf away from the chocolate.

Before turning out the charlotte, trim the sponge fingers to the level of the chocolate filling. Invert onto a serving plate and decorate with the whipped cream and chocolate leaves.
Serves 6

Gooseberry Ginger Crunch

8 gingernuts, crushed
25 g (1 oz) butter,
   melted
500 g (1 lb)
   gooseberries
1 tablespoon water
125 g (4 oz) caster
   sugar
1 egg white, stiffly
   whisked
284 ml (10 fl oz)
   double cream
few drops of green
   food colouring

Combine the gingernut crumbs and butter and leave on one side.

Place the gooseberries and water in a pan, cover and simmer for 15 minutes, until the fruit has pulped. Sieve or work in an electric blender until smooth. Stir in the sugar and leave to cool.

Fold the egg white into the gooseberry purée with the whipped cream and food colouring.

Divide half this mixture between glass serving dishes and sprinkle over half the gingernut mixture; repeat these layers. Chill well before serving.
Serves 6

Apple Amber

PASTRY:
175 g (6 oz) plain flour
75 g (3 oz) butter or margarine
1-2 tablespoons iced water

FILLING:
25 g (1 oz) butter
500 g (1 lb) cooking apples, peeled, cored and sliced
175 g (6 oz) caster sugar
1 teaspoon ground cinnamon
2 eggs, separated

Make pastry as for Individual Fish Flans (page 22) and use to line a 20 cm (8 inch) fluted flan ring. Line with greaseproof paper and dried beans and bake for 15 minutes. Remove the paper and beans and return to the oven for 5 minutes. Remove the flan ring and cool on a wire rack.

Melt the butter in a pan and add the apples. Cover and cook over low heat until pulped. Beat in 75 g (3 oz) sugar, the cinnamon and egg yolks.

Pour into the flan case and bake in a preheated moderate oven, 180°C (350°F), Gas Mark 4, for 15 minutes. Lower the oven temperature to 140°C (275°F), Gas Mark 1.

Whisk the egg whites stiffly, then whisk in half the remaining sugar. Fold in the rest and pile the meringue over the apple. Return to the oven for 1 hour or until meringue is crisp.
Serves 6

Fruit Meringue Baskets

4 egg whites
250 g (8 oz) caster sugar
284 ml (10 fl oz) whipping cream
50 g (2 oz) icing sugar
1 tablespoon liqueur (optional)
750 g (1½ lb) fresh or frozen and thawed soft fruit (e.g. raspberries, strawberries, cherries)

Mark six 10 cm (4 inch) circles on silicone paper. Place on oiled baking sheets and brush the paper with oil.

Whisk the egg whites until stiff. Add half the sugar and continue whisking until the mixture is smooth. Fold in the remaining sugar. Spread two-thirds of the meringue over the circles to form bases. Pipe the rest around the edges to make rims.

Bake in a preheated very cool oven, 120°C (250°F), Gas Mark ½, for 2 hours, until dry and crisp. Remove the paper and cool on a wire rack.

Whip the cream with the icing sugar and liqueur, if using. Fold in the fruit, reserving a few pieces. Pile into the baskets and decorate with reserved fruit.
Serves 6

BARBECUES

In the summer, the garden can be used almost as an extra room and one of the most informal ways of entertaining – the barbecue – can be used to its full advantage. The boy scout open wood fire and burned bangers are things of the past: many of the modern barbecues are very sophisticated and give an elegant approach to this casual form of cooking.

Advance preparation is essential. Meat can be marinated overnight for fullest flavour and tenderness. Salads can be kept crisp in the refrigerator with separate dressings at the ready for last-minute tossing. Keep the food to be barbecued as simple as possible, especially if you're a beginner. Have a plentiful supply of foil to make parcels of food, which should prevent charring. Flavoured butters help to keep food moist and add a delicious flavour. Drinks should be light and inexpensive – a wine or cider punch is ideal.

Site the barbecue with plenty of space around it so guests can participate in the cooking if they want to. Light the fire an hour before cooking begins to allow the charcoal to get to the 'glowing' stage – the charcoal should look ash-grey by daylight and glow red in the dark when it is ready. A sturdy table is useful for cooking utensils and basting sauces. Children love a barbecue, but do make sure they are supervised while cooking their food.

There is nothing more inviting than the aroma of food cooking in the open. Unfortunately, the only thing that cannot be controlled is the weather, so make sure you can move the party inside and pop foods under the grill if necessary.

Menu 1 for eight

Prawn chowder

Chicken liver and
kidney kebabs
Orange spare ribs
Green salad with
avocado
Pitta bread

Spiced bananas
Toasted marshmallows

Menu 2 for eight

Chilled sherried
grapefruit

Hamburgers with blue
cheese
Lemon chicken
Sweet and sour sauce
Sesame buns

Apple streusel pie

Prawn Chowder

125 g (4 oz) streaky
   bacon, derinded
   and chopped
4 potatoes, chopped
1 large onion, finely
   chopped
25 g (1 oz) plain
   flour
½ teaspoon curry
   powder
600 ml (1 pint) water
salt and pepper
250 g (8 oz) peeled
   prawns, fresh,
   canned and
   drained, or frozen
   and thawed
600 ml (1 pint) milk
4 tablespoons dry
   sherry (optional)
2 tablespoons
   chopped parsley to
   garnish

Place the bacon in a large pan and heat gently until the fat runs. Increase the heat and when the bacon begins to brown, add the potatoes and onion. Fry for 5 minutes, then stir in the flour and curry powder. Gradually add the water, stirring constantly. Season with salt and pepper to taste and bring to the boil, stirring. Add the prawns and simmer for 30 minutes, until the potato is tender.

Pour in the milk and sherry, if using, and heat through gently. Check the seasoning and sprinkle with chopped parsley just before serving.
Serves 8

Chilled Sherried Grapefruit

Prepare this refreshing starter a few hours before the barbecue, for convenience.

4 grapefruit
125 g (4 oz)
   demerara sugar
4 tablespoons sherry

Halve the grapefruit, loosen the segments with a serrated knife and snip out the core with scissors. Sprinkle 15 g (½ oz) of the sugar and ½ tablespoon of the sherry over each half.

Cover the grapefruit halves with cling film and chill for at least 1 hour before serving.
Serves 8

Chicken Liver and Kidney Kebabs

3 × 227 g (8 oz)
  tubs frozen chicken
  livers, thawed
16 lambs' kidneys,
  skinned, halved
  and cored
bay leaves to taste
salt and pepper
3 tablespoons oil

Thread the livers, kidneys and bay leaves alternately onto 8 skewers. Sprinkle with salt and pepper and brush with oil.

Place the kebabs on the barbecue grid, about 10 cm (4 inches) above the coals, and cook for about 10 minutes, turning frequently.
Serves 8

Green Salad with Avocado

1 lettuce
1 bunch watercress
½ cucumber, sliced
1 green pepper, cored,
  seeded and sliced
1 avocado pear
2 tablespoons lemon
  juice
4 tablespoons olive
  oil
1 teaspoon sugar
salt and pepper

Tear the lettuce into pieces and place in a salad bowl. Divide the watercress into sprigs and add to the bowl with the cucumber and green pepper. Peel the avocado, halve and remove the stone. Cut the avocado into slices just before serving, add to the salad and toss well.

Whisk together the lemon juice, oil, sugar, and salt and pepper to taste. Pour over the salad; toss well.
Serves 8

Orange Spare Ribs

1.5 kg (3 lb) pork
  spare ribs
2 tablespoons clear
  honey
1 tablespoon lemon
  juice
1 tablespoon
  Worcestershire
  sauce
1 teaspoon soy sauce
2 oranges
salt and pepper

Cut the spare ribs into serving pieces. Place the honey, lemon juice, Worcestershire sauce and soy sauce in a small pan. Grate the rind from one orange and add to the pan, together with the juice of both oranges. Add salt and pepper to taste and heat gently, stirring occasionally. Leave to cool, then pour over the meat. Leave to marinate overnight.

Drain and reserve the marinade. Place the spare ribs in a roasting pan and cook in a preheated moderate oven, 180°C (350°F), Gas Mark 4, for 1 hour.

Transfer to the barbecue grid, about 10 cm (4 inches) above the coals. Cook for 15 minutes, turning and basting frequently with the reserved marinade, until crisp.
Serves 8

Hamburgers with Blue Cheese

1 kg (2 lb) ground
  beef
1 onion, grated
1 egg, beaten
salt and pepper
125 g (4 oz) Danish
  blue cheese
50 g (2 oz) butter
8 sesame seed buns,
  split

Place the beef, onion, egg, and salt and pepper to taste in a bowl. Stir to bind well, then shape into 8 flat burgers. Cream the cheese and butter together.

Place the burgers on the barbecue grid, about 10 cm (4 inches) above the coals. Cook for about 10 minutes on each side.

Top the burgers with the cheese butter and sandwich them between the split sesame seed buns. Serve immediately.

Serves 8

Lemon Chicken

Serve this tasty dish with Sweet and sour sauce (below).

8 chicken pieces or
    16 drumsticks
2 lemons
125 g (4 oz) butter
1 clove garlic, crushed
salt and pepper

Make small cuts in the chicken flesh. Brush all over with the juice of one of the lemons. Grate the rind finely and squeeze the juice from the other lemon, then cream together with the butter, garlic, and salt and pepper to taste. Spread a little of the mixture on each piece of chicken and wrap in foil.

Place on the barbecue grid, about 15 cm (6 inches) above the coals, and cook for about 25 minutes. Lower the grid to about 10 cm (4 inches).

Remove the foil from the chicken and place on the lowered grid. Cook for a further 10 to 15 minutes, until the skin is crisp and the chicken is cooked through.
Serves 8

Sweet and Sour Sauce

Prepare this sauce ahead and reheat before serving, with Lemon Chicken (above) or other barbecued meats.

4 tablespoons oil
2 cloves garlic, crushed
2 onions, finely
    chopped
2 green peppers, cored,
    seeded and sliced
4 carrots, thinly sliced
2.5 cm (1 inch) piece
    root ginger, chopped
6 tablespoons white
    wine vinegar
300 ml (½ pint)
    water
50 g (2 oz) demerara
    sugar
1 tablespoon soy
    sauce
2 tablespoons
    cornflour
salt and pepper

Heat the oil in the frying pan, add the garlic, onions, green peppers, carrots and ginger and fry for about 2 minutes until softened.

Place the remaining ingredients in a bowl, with salt and pepper to taste. Mix thoroughly until smooth, then add to the vegetables. Bring to the boil, stirring, then simmer for 20 minutes until the vegetables are tender and the sauce is thickened.

Serve hot with barbecued meats.
Makes about 900 ml (1½ pints)

Spiced Bananas

8 bananas
2 tablespoons lemon
  juice
8 tablespoons soft
  brown sugar
50 g (2 oz) butter
1 teaspoon cinnamon

Place each banana on a double piece of foil. Brush well with the lemon juice and sprinkle 1 tablespoon sugar on each. Cream together the butter and cinnamon and divide between the bananas, dotting along the top.

Wrap each banana securely and cook on the barbecue grid, about 10 cm (4 inches) above the coals, for about 10 minutes. Unwrap and serve hot, on the foil.
Serves 8

Toasted Marshmallows

An ideal treat to include in your barbecue for children.

2 packets
  marshmallows

Spear one marshmallow at a time onto a kebab skewer or clean stick. Hold over the barbecue, turning frequently, until puffed up and golden. Serve immediately.
Serves 8

Apple Streusel Pie

250 g (8 oz) plain
  flour
125 g (4 oz) butter
1 tablespoon icing
  sugar
1 egg yolk
2 tablespoons cold
  water

FILLING:
1 kg (2 lb) cooking
  apples, peeled,
  cored and sliced
50 g (2 oz) raisins
125 g (4 oz) plain
  flour
125 g (4 oz) caster
  sugar
50 g (2 oz) butter
284 ml (10 fl oz)
  double cream

TOPPING:
50 g (2 oz) caster
  sugar
2 teaspoons cinnamon

Sift the flour into a bowl and rub in
the butter until the mixture resembles
breadcrumbs. Stir in the icing sugar
and bind together with the egg yolk
and water. Roll out the pastry thinly
and use to line two 18 cm (7 inch) or
one 25 cm (10 inch) flan tin.

To make the filling, mix the apples
and raisins together. Sift the flour
into a bowl and stir in the sugar. Rub
in the butter, using the fingertips.
Spoon half the rubbed-in mixture
into the flan. Cover with the apples
and raisins, then pour over the
cream. Spoon over the remaining
rubbed-in mixture and sprinkle with
the topping.

Bake in a preheated moderately
hot oven, 200°C (400°F), Gas Mark 6,
for 25 minutes, then reduce the heat
to 190°C (375°F), Gas Mark 5, and
cook for a further 10 minutes. Serve
hot or cold.

Serves 8

BUFFET LUNCHES & SUPPERS

The thought of catering for 20 or 30 guests is enough to scare many people, but with careful planning and a little time, it should not prove much different from catering for a family.

Choose the menu about a month before and spread the cost and volume shopping over a period. Buy the largest packs of foods available – they work out much cheaper. Think about the visual impact of the whole buffet – the shapes of dishes and garnishes – and include a variety of textures. The use of a freezer comes into its own when catering for large numbers. Many stages of dishes can be completed and frozen and the buffet put together one or two days before.

There's no need to buy large cooking utensils for the party: a preserving pan can be used for making soups and cooking large quantities of rice and vegetables; roasting pans can be covered with a double layer of foil and used as casseroles. Guests will not expect you to have 30 matching place settings so borrow, hire or use disposable plates, etc.

Brunch menu for twelve

Florida salad

Kedgeree
Bacon and sausage kebabs
Devilled kidneys
Soda bread
Blinis

Maple and walnut muffins

Lunch menu for twenty

Vichyssoise

Gammon with Cumberland sauce
Herb bread
Red cabbage salad
Bean and sweetcorn salad

Chocolate and apricot gâteau

Summer wine punch

Entertaining large numbers at lunchtime is generally confined to weekends. For those able to enjoy a late start to the day, a breakfast-type lunch party is just the right meal: the 'brunch' menu (see opposite) is ideal. The American-style hot buffet supper is quite economical and ideal for a teenage party.

Supper menu for twenty★

Bacon and pizza fingers
Chilli dogs
Boston baked beans
Thousand island salad

Banana ice cream
Peanut brownies

Cider cup

Supper menu for thirty

Skordalia

Circassian chicken
Pilaff
Tomato and cucumber salad

Orange halva cake
Yogurt with dried fruit

Supper menu for twenty★

Rabbit terrine
Mustard bread

Turkey tonnato
Potato salad
Crispy lettuce and cauliflower salad
Broad bean and carrot salad

Hazelnut meringue layer
Paris brest with ginger

Supper menu for thirty

Blushing eggs

Pissaladière
Quiche Lorraine
Onion quiche
Coleslaw with pineapple

Fluffy lemon trifle

Florida Salad

3 pink grapefruit
3 white grapefruit
6 oranges
1 cantaloup melon
175 g (6 oz) caster
   sugar
2 tablespoons lemon
   juice

Peel the citrus fruits and remove the segments with a sharp knife, discarding all pith. Place in a serving bowl. Halve the melon and remove the seeds. Cut the flesh into neat cubes and add to the bowl. Sprinkle with the caster sugar and lemon juice and chill before serving.
Serves 12

Kedgeree

1 kg (2 lb) smoked
   haddock fillets
150 ml (¼ pint)
   milk
125 g (4 oz) butter
300 g (10 oz) easy-
   cook Italian rice
salt and pepper
4 eggs, hard-boiled
1 tablespoon chopped
   parsley to garnish

Place the haddock in a pan with the milk and half the butter. Bring to the boil, then poach for 10 minutes. Remove the skin and any bones and flake the fish.

Cook the rice in plenty of boiling salted water for about 10 minutes, until just tender.

Chop two of the eggs. Cut the other two in half, remove and sieve the yolks and chop the whites; set aside for garnish.

Melt the remaining butter in a pan and stir in the fish, rice and chopped eggs. Heat gently for 5 minutes.

Transfer to a warmed serving dish and garnish with the sieved egg yolk, chopped egg white and chopped parsley. Serve immediately.
Serves 12

Bacon and Sausage Kebabs

1 kg (2 lb) streaky
   bacon, derinded
1 kg (2 lb) cocktail
   sausages
350 g (12 oz) button
   mushrooms
7 tablespoons cooking
   oil (approximately)
salt and pepper
parsley sprigs to
   garnish

Cut each rasher in half and roll up each piece tightly. Thread the sausages, bacon and mushrooms alternately on 12 skewers. Brush with oil and sprinkle with salt and pepper. Cook under a preheated moderate grill for about 10 minutes, turning frequently and brushing with more oil as necessary. Serve hot, garnished with parsley.
Serves 12

Devilled Kidneys

12 lambs' kidneys
75 g (3 oz) butter
3 onions, chopped
450 ml (¾ pint) beef
  stock
2 tablespoons Meaux
  mustard
1 tablespoon
  Worcestershire
  sauce
salt and pepper
TO GARNISH:
3 slices bread, crusts
  removed
oil for shallow frying
1 tablespoon chopped
  parsley

Skin, core and halve the kidneys.

Melt 25 g (1 oz) of the butter in a pan, add the onions and fry until golden brown. Add the stock, mustard, Worcestershire sauce, and salt and pepper to taste. Bring to the boil and simmer until well reduced.

Melt the remaining butter in a separate pan, add the kidneys and fry for 5 minutes, turning occasionally. Pour over the sauce and heat through while preparing the garnish.

Cut the bread slices into triangles. Fry in a little oil until golden brown.

To serve, transfer the kidneys to a warmed serving dish, sprinkle with the parsley and surround with the bread triangles.

Serves 12

Soda Bread

500 g (1 lb)
wholewheat flour
250 g (8 oz) plain
flour
1 teaspoon sugar
1 teaspoon salt
2 teaspoons
bicarbonate of soda
500 ml (18 fl oz)
buttermilk
2 tablespoons milk to
glaze

Sift the dry ingredients into a bowl.
Make a well in the centre and pour in
the buttermilk. Stir the flour in from
the side and knead lightly until
smooth. Divide the dough in half
and shape into 2 rounds.

Place on a greased baking sheet
and mark each round into quarters,
using a sharp knife. Brush with milk
and bake in a preheated hot oven,
220°C (425°F), Gas Mark 7, for 25 to
30 minutes.

Serve with butter and preserves or
honey.

Serves 12

NOTE: If buttermilk is unobtainable,
use half milk and half natural low-fat
yogurt instead.

Blinis

150 ml (¼ pint)
  warm milk
½ tablespoon dried
  yeast
1 teaspoon sugar
175 g (6 oz)
  buckwheat or
  plain flour
2 eggs, separated
oil or butter for
  frying
TO SERVE:
1 × 56 g (2 oz) jar
  lumpfish roe
125 g (4 oz) smoked
  salmon pieces
300 ml (½ pint)
  soured cream
½ bunch spring
  onions, chopped

Blend the milk with the yeast and
sugar; leave to stand for 10 minutes.

Sift the flour into a bowl, make a
well in the centre and gradually beat
in the milk mixture, then the egg
yolks. Cover and leave in a warm
place for 1 hour. Whisk the egg
whites stiffly and fold into the batter.

Oil or butter a heavy-based pan
and place over a moderate heat.
Drop tablespoons of the batter into
the pan and fry quickly, turning
once. Remove from the pan and keep
warm under a cloth while cooking
the remaining batter.

To serve, spread half the blinis
with lumpfish roe, and top the rest
with smoked salmon pieces. Serve
warm, with the soured cream and
spring onions in separate bowls.
Serves 12

Maple and Walnut Muffins

175 g (6 oz)
    self-raising flour
1 teaspoon salt
75 g (3 oz) walnut
    pieces, chopped
5 tablespoons maple-
    flavoured syrup
5 tablespoons water
40 g (1½ oz) butter
1 egg, beaten

Sift the flour and salt into a bowl and stir in the walnuts. Make a well in the centre.

Place the syrup, water and butter in a pan and heat gently, stirring, until the butter has melted. Pour into the well in the flour mixture and beat thoroughly. Beat in the egg to give a smooth batter.

Line a 12-hole bun tin with paper cases. Spoon in the batter to two-thirds fill the cases. Bake in a preheated moderately hot oven, 190°C (375°F), Gas Mark 5, for 20 minutes, until risen and firm to touch. Transfer to a wire rack to cool slightly.

Serve warm, split and buttered.
Makes 12

Vichyssoise

75 g (3 oz) butter
350 g (12 oz)
  onions, chopped
1.5 kg (3 lb) leeks,
  sliced
750 g (1½ lb)
  potatoes, sliced
3.5 litres (6 pints)
  chicken stock
284 ml (10 fl oz)
  single cream
salt and pepper
chopped chives or
  spring onion tops
  to garnish

Melt the butter in a large pan, add the onions and fry gently until translucent but not browned. Add the leeks and fry for 5 minutes. Add the potatoes and stock. Bring to the boil, cover and simmer for 30 minutes.

Cool slightly, then sieve or work in an electric blender until smooth. Transfer to a large bowl or soup tureen, stir in the cream and season with salt and pepper to taste. Chill.

Sprinkle with chopped chives or spring onion tops to serve.
Serves 20

Gammon with Cumberland Sauce

1 gammon, on the
  bone, weighing
  about 4.5 kg
  (10 lb)
4 bay leaves
1 tablespoon black
  peppercorns
1 onion
8 cloves
175 g (6 oz) dried
  breadcrumbs
SAUCE:
2 oranges
2 lemons
1 × 454 g (1 lb) jar
  redcurrant jelly
150 ml (¼ pint) port
TO GARNISH:
1 orange, sliced and
  twisted
watercress sprigs

Place the gammon in a large pan with the bay leaves, peppercorns and onion studded with the cloves. Cover with cold water, bring to the boil and skim the surface. Simmer for about 3½ hours, allowing 20 minutes per 500 g (1 lb) plus 20 minutes over. Leave to cool in the cooking liquid.

Meanwhile prepare the sauce. Peel the rind thinly from the oranges and lemons and cut into fine shreds. Cover with cold water, bring to the boil and boil for 2 minutes; drain.

Squeeze the juice from the fruit, place in a pan with the redcurrant jelly and heat gently, stirring, until the jelly melts. Simmer for 5 minutes, then add the port and shredded rind. Leave to cool.

Remove skin from the gammon and press the breadcrumbs into the fat. Carve and arrange on a serving platter. Garnish with orange twists and watercress. Serve with the sauce.
Serves 20

Herb Bread

450 ml (¾ pint)
    warm milk
1 tablespoon dried
    yeast
1 teaspoon black
    treacle
1 tablespoon dried
    mixed herbs
350 g (12 oz) plain
    flour
2 teaspoons salt
350 g (12 oz)
    wholemeal flour
25 g (1 oz) butter

Mix together the milk, yeast, treacle
and herbs; set aside for 10 minutes.

Sift the plain flour and salt into a
bowl, then stir in the wholemeal
flour. Rub in the butter. Add the
milk mixture; mix to a firm dough.

Turn onto a floured surface and
knead for 5 minutes until smooth
and elastic. Place in a clean bowl,
cover with a damp tea-towel and
leave to rise in a warm place for
1 hour or until doubled in size.

Turn onto a floured surface and
knead again for a few minutes. Cut
in half and either place in two 500 g
(1 lb) greased loaf tins, or shape into
rounds and put on greased baking
sheets. Leave to rise in a warm place
for 30 minutes.

Bake in a preheated hot oven, 230°C
(450°F), Gas Mark 8, for 30 minutes
or until the loaves sound hollow
when tapped. Cool on a wire rack.
Serves 20

Red Cabbage Salad

1 red cabbage
1 cucumber
350 g (12 oz)
    tomatoes
350 g (12 oz) dessert
    apples
juice of 2 lemons
8 tablespoons olive
    oil
salt and pepper

Shred the cabbage finely. Slice the cucumber and tomatoes. Slice the apples, discarding the cores.

Put the prepared vegetables and fruit in a salad bowl. Whisk together the lemon juice, oil and salt and pepper to taste. Pour over the salad and toss well.
Serves 20

Bean and Sweetcorn Salad

350 g (12 oz) dried
    red kidney beans
2 × 326 g (11½ oz)
    cans sweetcorn,
    drained
1 large onion, thinly
    sliced
120 ml (4 fl oz)
    French dressing
2 tablespoons chopped
    parsley to garnish

Soak the beans in cold water overnight. Drain, place in a pan, cover with fresh cold water and bring to the boil. Boil rapidly for 10 minutes, then simmer for 45 minutes. Drain and cool.

Place in a salad bowl, add the sweetcorn, onion and French dressing and toss well to mix. Sprinkle with the chopped parsley just before serving.
Serves 20

Chocolate and Apricot Gâteau

For a buffet lunch to serve twenty, make two gâteaux.

300 g (10 oz) plain
  flour
50 g (2 oz) cocoa
  powder
½ teaspoon salt
4 teaspoons baking
  powder
300 g (10 oz) soft
  brown sugar
4 eggs, separated
175 ml (6 fl oz) corn
  oil
175 ml (6 fl oz) milk
1 teaspoon vanilla
  essence
FILLING AND
  TOPPING:
1 × 411 g (14½ oz)
  can apricot halves
2 tablespoons rum or
  apricot liqueur
½ × 340 g (12 oz)
  jar apricot conserve
284 ml (10 fl oz)
  whipping cream,
  whipped
25 g (1 oz) plain
  chocolate

Sift the flour, cocoa, salt and baking powder into a bowl. Stir in the sugar, then add the egg yolks, oil, milk and vanilla essence. Beat well until smooth. Whisk the egg whites and fold into the mixture.

Pour into a lined and greased 25 cm (10 inch) deep cake tin and bake in a preheated moderate oven, 180°C (350°F), Gas Mark 4, for 50 minutes to 1 hour until risen and firm to the touch. Leave in the tin.

Drain the juice from the apricots into a small pan. Add the rum or liqueur and heat gently. Pour all over the top of the cake and leave in the tin until cold, then remove.

Split the cake in half and sandwich together with the apricot conserve. Place the cake on a serving plate and cover completely with the cream, spreading it on with a palette knife.

Arrange the apricots cut side down around the top edge of the cake.

Using a potato peeler, peel the chocolate to make curls. Sprinkle over the top of the cake to complete the decoration.
Serves 10

Summer Wine Punch

4 bottles hock
1 bottle dry sherry
1.5 litres (2½ pints)
  lemonade
ice cubes
2 mint sprigs
1 apple, quartered,
  cored and sliced
125 g (4 oz)
  strawberries
  (optional)

Mix the wine and sherry and divide between jugs. Top up with lemonade and ice cubes. Top with mint, apple and sliced strawberries if using.
Makes 30 glasses
NOTE: Any medium white wine may be used in place of hock.

Bacon and Pizza Fingers

1 × 567 g (20 oz)
  packet white bread
  mix
75 g (3 oz) butter
500 g (1 lb) onions,
  chopped
4 cloves garlic,
  crushed
2 × 397 g (14 oz)
  cans chopped
  tomatoes
2 teaspoons dried
  mixed herbs
salt and pepper
500 g (1 lb) streaky
  bacon, derinded

Make up the bread mix according to packet instructions. Divide in half. Roll out each piece to fit a 35 × 25 cm (14 × 10 inch) greased baking sheet.

Melt the butter in a pan, add the onions and garlic and fry until translucent. Spread over the dough.

Mix the tomatoes and juice with the herbs and salt and pepper to taste, then spread over the onions. Top with the bacon.

Bake in a preheated hot oven, 230°C (450°F), Gas Mark 8, for 10 minutes. Lower the heat to 180°C (350°F), Gas Mark 4, and bake for 30 minutes.

Serve warm, cut into fingers.
Serves 20

Chilli Dogs

20 hot dog sausages
20 long bread rolls
SAUCE:
50 g (2 oz) butter
3 onions, finely
  chopped
1 × 793 g (1 lb 12 oz)
  can tomatoes
2 teaspoons Tabasco
1 × 65 g (2¼ oz)
  can tomato purée
salt and pepper

First prepare the sauce. Melt the butter in a pan, add the onions and cook gently until soft. Add the tomatoes with their juice and the remaining ingredients, with salt and pepper to taste. Simmer for about 20 minutes, until thickened.

Meanwhile, cook the sausages according to instructions. Split the rolls and put a sausage in each. Pour a little sauce over each hot dog.
Serves 20

Boston Baked Beans

500 g (1 lb) haricot
    beans
350 g (12 oz) streaky
    bacon, chopped
3 onions, chopped
2 teaspoons mustard
    powder
1 tablespoon brown
    sugar
2 tablespoons black
    treacle
1 × 142 g (5 oz)
    can tomato purée
salt and pepper

Rinse the beans, cover with cold water and soak overnight. Drain, cover with fresh cold water and bring to the boil. Boil rapidly for 10 minutes, then drain.

Put the beans, bacon and onions in a casserole and add water to cover. Stir in remaining ingredients, adding 2 teaspoons salt, and pepper to taste.

Cover and cook in a preheated cool oven, 150°C (300°F), Gas Mark 2, for 5 to 6 hours, stirring occasionally and adding more water if necessary.
Serves 20

Thousand Island Salad

3 round lettuce
2 bunches watercress
1 cucumber
1 kg (2 lb) tomatoes
DRESSING:
500 g (1.1 lb) jar
    mayonnaise
1 tablespoon stuffed
    olives, chopped
½ green pepper, cored,
    seeded and chopped
1 small onion, grated
1 tablespoon chopped
    parsley
2 teaspoons tomato
    purée

Tear the lettuce into small pieces and the watercress into sprigs. Divide between 2 large salad bowls. Slice the cucumber and tomatoes and add to the bowls. Toss together well to mix.

Place the dressing ingredients in a bowl and stir well until thoroughly combined.

Transfer to a sauce bowl and serve separately.
Serves 20

Banana Ice Cream

450 ml (¾ pint)
  milk
175 g (6 oz) caster
  sugar
3 eggs, beaten
1 teaspoon vanilla
  essence
450 ml (¾ pint)
  double cream
6 bananas, mashed

Put the milk, sugar and eggs in a
small pan and heat gently, stirring
constantly, until the mixture
thickens. Strain into a bowl and add
the vanilla essence. Leave to cool.
  Whip the cream until slightly
thickened and fold into the cooled
custard. Stir in the mashed bananas.
Pour into a rigid freezerproof container,
cover, seal and freeze until firm.
  Transfer to the refrigerator about
1 hour before serving to soften.
Transfer to a large chilled glass dish
to serve.
Serves 20

Peanut Brownies

50 g (2 oz) cocoa
  powder
125 g (4 oz) butter,
  melted
250 g (8 oz) caster
  sugar
3 eggs, beaten
125 g (4 oz) self-
  raising flour, sifted
125 g (4 oz)
  unsalted peanuts,
  chopped

Stir the cocoa powder into the melted
butter. Put the sugar, eggs, flour and
peanuts into a mixing bowl, pour
over the butter mixture and beat
together thoroughly for 3 minutes.
  Pour the mixture into a lined and
greased oblong cake tin, 28 × 18 cm
(11 × 7 inches). Bake in a preheated
moderate oven, 180°C (350°F), Gas
Mark 4, for 30 to 40 minutes until
firm.
  Cut into 20 squares and transfer to
a wire rack to cool.
Makes 20

Cider Cup

4.5 litres (8 pints)
  dry cider
1 × 1 litre (1.76 pint)
  carton pineapple
  juice
1 litre (1¾ pints)
  lemonade
1 orange, sliced
1 lemon, sliced
1 tray ice cubes

Chill the cider, pineapple juice and
lemonade separately. Just before
serving, pour all three into a large
bowl and float the orange and lemon
slices and ice cubes on the top.
Makes about 40 glasses
NOTE: Decorate individual servings
with mint leaves if liked.

Skordalia

SAUCE:
8 egg yolks
12 fat cloves garlic,
   crushed
600 ml (1 pint) olive
   oil
250 g (8 oz) ground
   almonds
250 g (8 oz) fresh
   breadcrumbs
2 tablespoons lemon
   juice
2 tablespoons
   chopped parsley
TO SERVE:
1 kg (2 lb) small
   courgettes
1 kg (2 lb) French
   beans
1 large cauliflower
salt
1 kg (2 lb) tomatoes
15 eggs, hard-boiled

Put 4 egg yolks and 6 garlic cloves in
an electric blender or food processor.
Switch on at full speed and trickle in
half the oil slowly until the mixture
is thick. Pour into a large bowl.

Repeat this process with the
remaining egg yolks, garlic and olive
oil, then add to the bowl. Add the
remaining ingredients and mix
together thoroughly. Divide
between 2 serving bowls.

Top and tail the courgettes and
beans. Break the cauliflower into
florets. Cook the vegetables
separately in boiling salted water for
a few minutes until just tender but
still firm. Drain and leave to cool.

Cut the courgettes lengthways
into sticks, tomatoes into quarters,
and the eggs in half lengthways.

Place the bowls of skordalia on
large platters and arrange the eggs
and vegetables around them to serve.
Serves 30

Pilaff

150 ml (¼ pint)
  sunflower oil
1 kg (2 lb)
  long-grain rice
1 litre (1¾ pints)
  water
4 teaspoons salt
500 g (1 lb) onions,
  chopped
6 fat cloves garlic,
  sliced
125 g (4 oz)
  blanched whole
  almonds
125 g (4 oz) raisins
500 g (1 lb) tomatoes,
  skinned, seeded
  and chopped

Heat 5 tablespoons of the oil in a
large pan and add the rice, water and
salt. Bring to the boil, cover tightly
and simmer for about 15 minutes,
until the liquid is absorbed and the
rice is tender.

Meanwhile, heat the remaining oil
in another pan, add the onions, garlic
and almonds and fry until golden.
Add the raisins and tomatoes and
cook for 5 minutes.

Transfer the rice to a large warmed
serving dish, flaking with a fork to
separate the grains. Pour the onion
and tomato mixture from the pan
over the rice and mix in with a fork
until well blended. Serve hot.
Serves 30
Illustrated on following page

Circassian Chicken

5 × 1.5 kg (3½ lb)
  chickens
5 carrots
5 onions, quartered
5 bouquet garni
salt and pepper
175 g (6 oz)
  hazelnuts
250 g (8 oz) walnut
  pieces
175 g (6 oz) butter
500 g (1 lb) onions,
  sliced
175 g (6 oz) ground
  almonds
1 kg (2.2 lb) carton
  natural low-fat
  yogurt
1 teaspoon paprika
watercress sprigs to
  garnish

Place each chicken in a pan with a carrot, onion, bouquet garni and salt and pepper to taste. Cover with cold water, bring to the boil, then simmer for 1½ hours. Leave in the cooking liquid until cool, then remove the skin and cut all flesh from the bones into pieces; set aside. Reserve 300 ml (½ pint) of the cooking liquid.

Grind the hazelnuts and 175 g (6 oz) of the walnuts; set aside.

Melt the butter in a large pan, add the remaining walnut pieces and fry until golden brown. Remove with a slotted spoon and set aside for garnish. Add the sliced onions to the pan and fry until soft but not brown.

Add the ground hazelnuts and walnuts to the pan with the ground almonds, yogurt, paprika and reserved stock. Add the chicken meat and heat through gently, stirring.

Transfer to a warmed serving dish, sprinkle with the walnuts and serve, garnished with watercress.
Serves 30

Tomato and Cucumber Salad

2 cucumbers
2 kg (4½ lb) tomatoes
250 g (8 oz) Lanca-
  shire cheese, grated
4 tablespoons chopped
  chives or parsley
DRESSING:
150 ml (¼ pint)
  olive oil
4 tablespoons white
  wine vinegar
1 teaspoon caster
  sugar
1 teaspoon mustard
  powder
2 cloves garlic, crushed
salt and pepper

Thinly slice the cucumbers and tomatoes into a large salad bowl. Sprinkle with the cheese and herbs.

Put all the dressing ingredients, with salt and pepper to taste, in a screw-top jar and shake well. Pour over the salad just before serving, tossing lightly.
Serves 30

Illustrated opposite: Circassian chicken; Pilaff; Tomato and cucumber salad

Orange Halva Cake

Make three of these cakes to serve thirty people.

CAKE MIXTURE:
175 g (6 oz) butter
175 g (6 oz) caster
   sugar
grated rind and juice
   of 1 orange
3 eggs, beaten
275 g (9 oz) semolina
125 g (4 oz) ground
   almonds
3 teaspoons baking
   powder

SYRUP:
175 g (6 oz) caster
   sugar
5 tablespoons water
2 tablespoons lemon
   juice
½ teaspoon ground
   cinnamon
25 g (1 oz) chopped
   candied peel
3 tablespoons orange
   juice

TO DECORATE:
142 ml (5 fl oz)
   whipping cream,
   whipped
25 g (1 oz) flaked
   almonds, toasted

Cream the butter and sugar together with the grated orange rind until pale and fluffy. Beat in the orange juice and eggs, then fold in the semolina, ground almonds and baking powder.

Turn into a greased and floured 23 cm (9 inch) ring tin. Bake in a preheated hot oven, 220°C (425°F), Gas Mark 7, for 10 minutes, then lower the heat to 180°C (350°F), Gas Mark 4, and bake for a further 30 minutes.

Meanwhile prepare the syrup. Place the sugar, water, lemon juice, cinnamon and peel in a pan and bring to the boil, stirring. Simmer until slightly thickened, then add the orange juice.

Turn the cake onto a serving plate straight from the oven. Pour the syrup over the hot cake slowly until it is all absorbed. Leave to cool.

To serve, fill the centre of the ring with the whipped cream and sprinkle the almonds on the cake.
Serves 10

Yogurt with Dried Fruit

1 kg (2.2 lb) carton
   natural low-fat
   yogurt
125 g (4 oz) mixed
   dried fruit,
   chopped (apricots,
   apples, peaches,
   prunes, etc.)
1 teaspoon ground
   cinnamon

Mix all the ingredients together in a serving bowl and chill for at least 3 hours.
Serves 30
NOTE: Ready-mixed dried fruit salad pieces are sold in packets.

Rabbit Terrine

175 g (6 oz) fresh
    breadcrumbs
450 ml (¾ pint)
    milk
1.5 kg (3 lb)
    boneless rabbit
750 g (1½ lb) pork
    fillet
3 eggs, beaten
2 teaspoons ground
    nutmeg
1 tablespoon Dijon
    mustard
salt and pepper
9 bay leaves
500 g (1 lb) streaky
    bacon, derinded
parsley sprigs to
    garnish

Soak the breadcrumbs in the milk for
10 minutes. Cut the rabbit and pork
into cubes and either mince coarsely
or chop in a food processor. Place in
a mixing bowl.

Strain the breadcrumbs. Add to the
meat with the eggs, nutmeg, mustard,
and salt and pepper to taste; mix well.

Place the bay leaves in three 1 litre
(1¾ pint) terrines. Line the terrines
with the bacon rashers, stretching
them to fit if necessary. Fill with the
meat mixture, pressing down firmly,
and cover with a lid or buttered foil.

Place in a roasting pan containing
water to come halfway up the sides
of the terrines and cook in a
preheated moderate oven, 180°C
(350°F), Gas Mark 4, for 2 hours.

Remove the terrines from the pan
and place a weight on top of each
one; leave to cool. Chill overnight.

Turn out onto a serving platter,
slice and garnish with parsley.
Serves 20

Mustard Bread

3 baguettes
500 g (1 lb) butter
1 small jar French or
  Dijon mustard

Split the baguettes in half lengthways. Cream the butter and mustard together until well blended. Spread thickly along the length of the loaves. Wrap in foil and bake in a preheated moderately hot oven, 200°C (400°F), Gas Mark 6, for 20 minutes.

Leave in the foil and slice thickly to serve.
Serves 20

Potato Salad

1.5 kg (3 lb) new
  potatoes
salt
1 bunch spring
  onions, sliced
2 celery sticks, finely
  sliced
1 × 500 g (1.1 lb)
  jar mayonnaise
1 tablespoon chopped
  parsley

Cook the potatoes in their skins in boiling salted water until cooked but still firm. Drain and carefully peel off skins, then dice. Place in a salad bowl with the spring onions and celery; add the mayonnaise and toss until the potatoes are well coated. Sprinkle with parsley to serve.
Serves 20

Illustrated on following page

Turkey Tonnato

2 turkey roasts, about
  1.5 kg (3 lb)
  each, or 1 ×
  4.5 kg (10 lb)
  oven-ready turkey
1 onion, sliced
1 carrot, sliced
1 bouquet garni
salt and pepper
SAUCE:
1 × 198 g (7 oz)
  can tuna fish,
  drained
1 × 50 g (1¾ oz)
  can anchovy
  fillets, drained
2 × 71 g (2½ oz)
  jars capers
3 tablespoons lemon
  juice
1 × 500 g (1.1 lb)
  jar mayonnaise

Place the turkey roasts or prepared turkey in a roasting pan. Pour in 300 ml (½ pint) water and add the onion, carrot, bouquet garni, and salt and pepper to taste. Cover the pan completely with foil and cook in a preheated moderate oven, 160°C (325°F), Gas Mark 3, for 2 hours for the turkey roasts and 3¾ hours for the turkey. Leave in the juices in the pan overnight to cool; reserve the juices next day.

Place the tuna fish, anchovies, one jar of capers with juice, and the lemon juice in an electric blender and blend until smooth. Add the mayonnaise and blend until well combined. If the sauce is too thick, mix in a little of the turkey stock.

Slice the turkey roast or carve the turkey, arrange on a large serving platter and coat with the sauce. Drain the remaining jar of capers and use to garnish the turkey.
Serves 20

Crispy Lettuce and Cauliflower Salad

2 red-skinned dessert
  apples
2 tablespoons lemon
  juice
1 large Iceberg
  lettuce, shredded
1 large cauliflower,
  broken into florets
6 slices garlic sausage,
  cut into strips
300 ml (½ pint)
  mayonnaise
142 ml (5 fl oz)
  soured cream
1 tablespoon curry
  powder

Cut the apples into quarters, remove the cores, then slice the apples thinly. Sprinkle the lemon juice over the apple slices to prevent browning. Place in a large salad bowl with the lettuce, cauliflower and sausage.

Blend the mayonnaise, soured cream and curry powder together in a small bowl. Pour over the salad just before serving, tossing well.
Serves 20

*Illustrated opposite: Turkey tonnato;
Crispy lettuce and cauliflower salad;
Potato salad; Broad bean and carrot
salad.*

Broad Bean and Carrot Salad

*1 kg (2 lb) frozen
  broad beans*
*250 g (8 oz) carrots,
  grated*
*150 ml (¼ pint)
  French dressing*
*1 tablespoon chopped
  chives*

Put the frozen broad beans in a bowl
and pour over boiling water to
cover; leave for 2 minutes, then drain
and pop off the skins. Mix with the
carrots in a serving bowl. Pour over
the French dressing and toss lightly.

  Sprinkle with chopped chives to
serve.

Serves 20

Hazelnut Meringue Layer

MERINGUE:
8 egg whites
500 g (1 lb) caster
   sugar
250 g (8 oz)
   hazelnuts, roasted
   and ground

FILLING:
600 ml (1 pint)
   double cream
1 × 220 g (7 oz) jar
   hazelnut chocolate
   spread

TO DECORATE:
50 g (2 oz) plain
   chocolate, melted
20 roasted hazelnuts

Place four of the egg whites in a bowl and whisk until stiff, then gradually whisk in 125 g (4 oz) of the sugar. Carefully fold in a further 125 g (4 oz) of the sugar and half of the ground nuts.

Spread the meringue into two 23 cm (9 inch) circles on a baking sheet lined with silicone paper. Repeat with the remaining meringue ingredients to make 4 rounds.

Bake them in a preheated cool oven, 140°C (275°F), Gas Mark 1, for 2½ hours until crisp. Carefully remove from the paper; cool on a wire rack.

Whip the cream and hazelnut spread together until it forms soft peaks. Using one-third of the cream, sandwich the meringues together in pairs to make 2 gâteaux. Spread another third of the cream over them.

Drizzle the chocolate on top of the gâteaux. Pipe on the remaining cream and top with the hazelnuts.
Makes two 23 cm (9 inch) gâteaux

Paris Brest with Ginger

CHOUX PASTRY:
300 ml (½ pint) water
125 g (4 oz) butter
150 g (5 oz) plain flour, sifted
½ teaspoon vanilla essence
4 eggs
50 g (2 oz) flaked almonds

FILLING:
125 g (4 oz) preserved ginger, chopped
284 ml (10 fl oz) whipping cream, whipped with 1 tablespoon syrup from the ginger

TO FINISH:
50 g (2 oz) icing sugar

Heat the water and butter slowly until the butter melts and the water just boils. Add the flour and beat until the mixture leaves the side of the pan. Cool slightly, then add the essence. Add three of the eggs to the mixture one at a time, beating well after each addition. Add the fourth egg gradually, reserving 1 spoonful.

Spoon the choux pastry into a 25 cm (10 inch) ring on a greased baking sheet. Brush with the reserved egg and sprinkle with the almonds. Bake in a preheated hot oven, 220°C (425°F), Gas Mark 7, for 15 minutes. Lower the heat to 190°C (375°F), Gas Mark 5 and bake for a further 25 minutes, until golden.

Split the cake horizontally. Scoop out any uncooked pastry and return the halves to the oven for 5 minutes.

Fold the ginger into the whipped cream and use to sandwich the cake together. Sprinkle with icing sugar.
Makes one 30 cm (10 inch) gâteau

Blushing Eggs

15 hard-boiled eggs
2 × 62.5 g (2.2 oz)
    packets creamy soft
    cheese
142 g (5 oz) can
    tomato purée
2 tablespoons
    mayonnaise
    (approximately)
salt and pepper
1 curly endive or
    lettuce, shredded
olive slices to garnish

Halve the eggs lengthwise, scoop out the yolks and place them in a basin with the cheese, tomato purée and mayonnaise. Beat well to give a soft piping consistency, adding more mayonnaise if necessary. Season with salt and pepper to taste. Pipe this mixture back into the eggs.

Serve on a bed of curly endive, or shredded lettuce, and garnish with olive slices.

Serves 30

Pissaladière

PASTRY:
500 g (1 lb) plain
  flour
250 g (8 oz)
  margarine
6 tablespoons water
FILLING:
75 g (3 oz) grated
  Parmesan cheese
3 tablespoons oil
3 onions, chopped
3 fat cloves garlic,
  crushed
1 × 793 g (1 lb 12
  oz) can tomatoes
1 × 397 g (14 oz)
  can tomatoes
1 × 65 g (2¼ oz)
  can tomato purée
salt and pepper
2 × 50 g (1¾ oz)
  cans anchovies,
  drained
125 g (4 oz) small
  black olives,
  halved and stoned

To make pastry, sift the flour into a bowl and rub in the margarine until the mixture resembles breadcrumbs. Add the water gradually and mix to a firm dough. Turn onto a lightly floured surface and knead lightly.

Divide the pastry into 3 pieces. Roll out and use to line three 20 cm (8 inch) flan tins. Line with greaseproof paper and dried beans and bake 'blind' in a preheated moderately hot oven, 200°C (400°F), Gas Mark 6, for 10 minutes. Remove paper and beans and return to the oven for 5 minutes. Sprinkle the bases with Parmesan.

Heat the oil in a pan, add the onions and garlic and fry gently until softened. Add the tomatoes with their juice, tomato purée, and salt and pepper to taste. Simmer for about 20 minutes, until thickened.

Divide between the flans and arrange the anchovies on top. Return to the oven for 10 minutes. Decorate with olives and serve hot or cold.
Serves 30

Quiche Lorraine

PASTRY:
500 g (1 lb) plain
  flour
250 g (8 oz)
  margarine
6 tablespoons water
FILLING:
350 g (12 oz) streaky
  bacon, derinded
  and chopped
175 g (6 oz) Cheddar
  cheese, grated
6 eggs, beaten
900 ml (1½ pints)
  milk
1 tablespoon mixed
  herbs
salt and pepper

Make the pastry as for Pissaladière (above). Divide into 3 equal pieces, roll out and use to line three 20 cm (8 inch) flan dishes or rings.

Bake blind (as for Pissaladière) in a preheated moderately hot oven, 200°C (400°F), Gas Mark 6, for 15 minutes.

Meanwhile, fry the bacon in its own fat over moderate heat until golden. Drain and divide between the cooked flan cases. Sprinkle with the cheese.

Beat together the eggs, milk, herbs, and salt and pepper to taste, and pour into the flan cases. Return to the oven for 25 minutes, or until golden and set. Serve hot or cold.
Serves 30

Onion Quiche

PASTRY:
*500 g (1 lb) plain
    flour*
*250 g (8 oz)
    margarine*
6 tablespoons water
FILLING:
175 g (6 oz) butter
*1.75 kg (4 lb)
    onions, sliced*
6 eggs
*175 g (6 oz)
    Cheddar cheese,
    grated*
salt and pepper

Make the pastry as for Pissaladière
(see page 91). Divide into 3 equal
pieces, roll out and use to line three
20 cm (8 inch) flan dishes or rings.

Melt the butter in a large pan, add
the onions, cover and cook gently
for about 30 minutes, until tender.

Remove from the heat and beat in
the eggs, then stir in the cheese and
salt and pepper to taste. Divide between the flan cases and bake in a preheated moderate oven, 180°C (350°F),
Gas Mark 4, for 30 minutes, until
golden and set. Serve hot or cold.
Serves 30

Coleslaw with Pineapple

1 large white cabbage,
  finely shredded
500 g (1 lb) carrots,
  grated
2 onions, grated
2 × 439 g (15½ oz)
  cans pineapple slices
250 g (8 oz) raisins
1 × 500 g (1.1 lb)
  jar mayonnaise
salt and pepper
chopped parsley to
  garnish

Mix the cabbage, carrots and onions together in a large salad bowl.

Drain the juice from the pineapple, reserving 150 ml (¼ pint). Cut the fruit into small pieces and add to the bowl with the raisins.

Blend the reserved pineapple juice with the mayonnaise and season with salt and pepper to taste. Pour over the salad and toss well to coat.

Sprinkle with chopped parsley to serve.
Serves 30

Fluffy Lemon Trifle

3 packets trifle
  sponge cakes
9 lemons
9 eggs, separated
3 × 397 g (14 oz)
  cans condensed
  milk
TO DECORATE:
284 ml (10 fl oz)
  double or whipping
  cream, whipped
125 g (4 oz) flaked
  almonds, toasted

Crumble the cakes into 3 large dishes. Grate the rind from 3 lemons and squeeze the juice from all of them.

Beat the egg yolks with the condensed milk, lemon rind and juice until thick and pale. Moisten the cake in each dish with 8 tablespoons of the mixture.

Whisk the egg whites until stiff and fold into the remaining lemon mixture. Pour over the sponge cakes and smooth the surface. Decorate with piped cream and flaked almonds.
Serves 30

INDEX